THE CANADIAN GIRL

THE CANADIAN GIRL

SHANNON STEWART

NIGHTWOOD EDITIONS

Published by
NIGHTWOOD EDITIONS
R.R.#5, S.26, C.13
Gibsons, BC Canada V0N 1V0

Cover design and illustration by Kim LaFave
Printed and bound in Canada
Nightwood Editions acknowledges the financial support of the Government of Canada through the Book Publishing Industry Development Program and the Province of British Columbia through the British Columbia Arts Council, for its publishing activities.

Canadian Cataloguing in Publication Data

Stewart, Shannon, 1966–
    The Canadian girl

    ISBN 0-88971-169-0

    I. Title.
PS8587.T4894C36 1998   C811'54   C98-911053-2
PR9199.3.S7945C36 1998

THE CANADA COUNCIL | LE CONSEIL DES ARTS
FOR THE ARTS | DU CANADA
SINCE 1957 | DEPUIS 1957

For my family

CONTENTS

THE CANADIAN GIRL

THE LOVES OF AUNT SOPHRONIA

TALKING TO GOD

GARDEN OF EARTHLY DELIGHTS

THE CANADIAN GIRL

THE CANADIAN GIRL 1937

"My great-grandmother had a chest
When she came here a bride;
She packed it for the journey west
With all the treasures she loved best
And locked her dreams inside."

Dorothy Brown Thompson

It hardly seems possible, this slim periodical
published by the United Church of Canada,
where girls say stuff like *Yoo-Hoo* and
Dad, you're a peach and give
their mothers swift pecks on the cheek.
But it's history after all,
this article on spring housecleaning;
salt and vinegar to clean your brass door knobs,
ammonia for the windows, mattresses aired
and pounded, carpets scrubbed, how to cope
with older brother's room filled with books
and radio appliances and how to have wieners
and baked beans on hand for a quick and easy
lunch. And that final warning for the zealots
among us – "Don't Bite Off More Than You Can Chew,"
because you might be in danger
of tearing up the whole house and who knew
what might happen then?

And there's an article on how to get rid
of your barnacles. Those being any strong
like or dislike, though here we concentrate
on the dislikes, fears of cats and stepladders
and doing, can you believe it, housework.

Barnacles, like the animals fastened to keels of ships,
slow you down.

Even the fear of bears is scorned, as seen
in the story of Kay, a girl who lives in the foothills of the Rockies.
One fine morning she walks out in search of the wildflowers
she paints beautifully in water colours and, mistaking a bear
for a clump of porcupines, comes eye to eye
with a grizzly, which does seem rather unlikely,
but we find out later the bear was on his back licking
the acid out of an old car battery he'd mistaken
for the formic acid in ants so now anything is
possible, in all this confusion. Kay calm
and fleet of foot, her father grabbing his gun
and giving pursuit, the bear turning a hand-spring
when he is shot, then lying still.

From the photo I can't imagine the thick-snouted
animal capable of a light trick before death,
but then I can't see large, placid Kay particularly
fleet of foot either. I suppose a bear who collapses
and a girl who gallumphs aren't as worthy of a story,
as the sensible girls are worthy, having written on
"The First Ten Books I'd Choose For My Library."
They select edifying and noble works;
Grammar at a Glance, Shakespeare and the Bible,
while the eccentric girl who wants *Peter Pan*,
Alice in Wonderland and a translation
of the Confucian Scriptures,
her letter is published last of all,
the last voice heard from in the paper,
above the subscription rates.

I think the editors were a little afraid of her,
I can see her spilling the contents of a house
in one fell swoop, burning the wieners and beans,
and terribly afraid of bears as anyone should be.
She'd march up to her great-grandmother's treasure chest
and throw it open, let all those dreams fly out,
the kind taken across the ocean

12

when you're coming to a new land,
which you think you can see though you're still
two days off, you're sixteen, you've got God
and a ship, and you swear you can see Canada,
just there, rising from the very last wave.

MY FATHER AND ARTICHOKES

He buys a bag of them in Chinatown, takes out the orange-glazed pot
at home where they bob and boil in a cloud of steam. The little dish of
butter sizzling in the center of the table, he shows me how to begin,
tearing off the leaves, scooping up butter, scraping the meat with my
teeth, careful of that single claw at the tip.

Watch it, he says. *That's the dangerous part.*

And he never tells me what I will find at the end. He keeps it secret
until I get there, the leaves turning pale and paper-thin until I come to
a core of fuzz to be scooped out with a knife. I think it is over, but
then he says:

This is the heart.

I quarter the round boat on my plate, perfectly empty and smooth, the
chipped outer edges where the shell has been peeled away, and I eat
the heartmeat, knowing this is what had to be protected, the
marrowed cup too delicate to reveal.

MY MOTHER AND ASPARAGUS

In her green coat, marching up the hill from the supermarket, the bundles of asparagus poking out from the brown paper bags. At home, she rolls off the red elastic and from the quiver of her white hand they spill like arrows across the table. She steams them in the coffee percolator, where they won't get bruised, stands them up gently, the swaying stalks of a forest pale before the storm, and through the thick glass bubble in the lid I see the tips burst into a green that doesn't belong to the kitchen, the dulled pots and counters and the sink full of dishes.

I am allowed to eat them with my fingers. She says it is the only way to eat asparagus, the spears across my plate, hot and buttery, my tongue finding the small nubs at the tips.

And later on, in the bathroom where she has just been, the smell of asparagus pee filling the small room, the musk of something gold and green and I imagine her there, the bright archer, crouched and ready, her eyes closed in the odour of it, the bow singing through fern and lily.

THE DIVINER

On nights of meteor showers my mother rolled her damp hair in
pincurls, smoothed her face with Revlon Moondrops, a yellow mask
promising the most beautiful skin. She'd lie on the picnic table, toes
pointing toward the eye of the moon widening over the island hills. I
could see her from the kitchen window as she read the winnowing sky,
the dropped flecks of light a body leaves upon falling to earth. The
silent mountain behind her where the dark wind took the birds into
sleep. I stood at the sink with a glass in my hand, contemplating the
water, my thirst, this ancient face brittle and golden, the soft skin I
knew to be beneath.

FISTS

The rabbit hunt. Funny
I don't remember
the crack of the gun,
the rabbit's body still and soft
the second before our father's finger
pulled the world a little tighter
into his hand.

What I do remember:
autumn coats, an uphill path.
The rabbit dangling
from long, veined ears.
My brother's grip
loosening, tightening, his face
like flour, the rabbit dropped
into the leaves. In and out
of breath before a fight, my father's
heavy boots in brush, his insistent
Pick it up. Keep going.
The boy and the man,
two players who had no choice
but to recite their angry lines.
Pink spot of fur where the soul
of the animal had been told to move out.
The smell in the cottage
that whole night, even after
the lights were shut, sweet as a room
of flowers only sweeter, wild meat
neither of us would taste
not because we didn't want to
but because we
wouldn't.

HAM

My brother stuck a piece of ham
in his ear because I dared him to.
We giggled and forgot about it.
Later his head began to stink.
Then came the doctors, the persistent
whys we couldn't begin to answer,
our plates taken away
as soon as we had eaten.

Children, orifices, the plumbed
depths of carnage.
It makes sense, doesn't it?
God pushed a thought into the void.
And it fit.

TARZAN AND ME

The year I learned
the language of the apes
I was nominated
blackboard cleaner.
Goro. The moon.
Numa. Lion.
Ara, usha, sheeta.
Lightning, wind and leopard.
At lunch hour I stood
in the school stairwell
clapping the chalk brushes,
whipping the golden shammy
through the air.
In that fine gilt powder
I dreamed him, Tarzan,
Lord of the Jungle,
where he moved
like a knot of rope
thrown against the sun.
A scarf of yellow silt
covered my hair.
I was precious.
I hung like a moth,
a touch could break my flight.

THE CASUALTIES

In school we'd seen a film about it,
the woman's cartoon body spilling its egg
down a white canal. It didn't
bother me a bit, though the smallest girl
in our class fainted.
Her mother hadn't told her a thing.

The night my period came
my parents had company over.
I remember the men's voices sliding
up and down the hall,
the women's laughter plucked and chilled,
getting into the corners of the house
where only the dust had settled.
As the blood fell like knotted silk
my mother stood over me,
in stockings and high heels,
saying she'd call the firetruck
if I didn't stop crying.

Why firetruck I'll never know.
Perhaps she was a little drunk
and the wailing red engine
made her think of me. Perhaps
she was angry, having told me
everything already, prepared me
as carefully as a roast,
trussed and glazed for the fire.
She could not understand the panic.
And I remember thinking
how I might just bleed to death
while my mother stood there
keen with wine and beauty
wearing pearls and gold
and her best perfume,
her lean calves arcing

like two white fish
from the floor.

Somewhere in the distance
there were sirens
and men in suits of armour
bright as poppies.
They carried the smallest girl
in their arms, the one
who didn't know what would happen to her.
They carried her high
like a medal across their chests,
my mother saying *hush, hush* –
the girl opening
her one perfect life.

DEAR MR. WRIGLEY

Gum-chewing was forbidden
in Mr. King's class.
The Jar
reminded us of this,
planted on his desk
like a malignant law.

After recess and lunch
our class filed in
dropping wads of gum
into the communal pot,
and behind the glass,
shining in a slick of gob,
Mr. King's brain-child,
a pink and green growth
of tyranny.

Terry Sawicki ratted on me,
having spied the Bubble-Yum
I immediately swallowed,
an act of cowardice
probably still
lodged in my stomach.
I walked to the front
of the class, where Mr. King
held The Jar out to me,
delighting in his best student's shame.

The boys hooted, the girls
grew calm and serious
and gave advice,
as only girls can
when one of their own
is about to fall.
The general consensus
was that I should choose
Bobby McGuire's gum,

floating on the top,
white and small and freshly
spat out.

I knew choice had nothing
to do with it, but the logic
was solid. My hand slipped
into The Jar, and from the oil
of thirty mouths I plucked
Bobby's gum, a pure snowflake
from the guts of the more
fruity flavours.

Maybe it was then
when our eyes first met,
or perhaps when I popped
the second-hand nugget
into my own mouth
and began the first
of twenty chews, as the class
roared and stamped their feet.

One girl told me
to stick it behind my teeth
and just pretend to chew.
But I was no cheater.
I bit into the gum
with gusto, Bobby watching me
and me watching him,
thinking the whole time...

we're in this together, Bobby McGuire.

Our saliva mixed in my mouth,
the boys hooting
for different reasons now,
the girls wary, Mr. King

worried he'd gone too far.
Bobby managing a sickly smile
of first love.

I'd like to write to Mr. Wrigley
tell him about my victory
in grade five,
and how out of punishment,
something rose and flew,
a clean little bird
on spearmint wings.

RENOVATIONS

We were on our knees
in the laundry room
tiling the floor.
My father moved beside me
spreading the patches of grout.
I fixed the tiles side by side,
wiping the edges clean.
I don't think
we said much.
It was enough to feel
the roughness of cement
under my hands, to hear
the furnace hissing and clicking
in a rhythm
I had not imagined
that hollow can
of green metal could keep.
And the washer and dryer gleaming
in the pure realm of my mother,
how their cold sides
groaned a little
when our shoulders bumped against them
in our work.
I liked this.
I wanted to be good and careful and quick
and my father must have seen it.
Must have known how hard
I was working to keep up
and it must have pained him,
his small daughter with his own
love and haste and sweat for the job,
knowing she knew the feel
of her palms and knees
on the dank floor, hovering
in the raw chemical smells of renovation,
Learning how true and fine
that could be with the radio voices

25

rolling across the bare room
and the bare light almost warm
on the back of her neck.
It must have pained him because he said
it wouldn't always be like this.
That one day I would turn sixteen
and selfish.
Boy-crazy, is what he said.
Too busy with boys
to help your father at night.
I stooped lower then,
the smell of the grout turning sour
and maybe he regretted
having said what he did
seeing me deny it, saying
No Never I won't
even then as that older girl
broached my side
like a curved bright hook between us.
I pressed the tiles
faster now, in neat rows,
willing them stuck forever,
as the furnace roared up behind us,
its warm breath
filling the rooms above.

THE LOVES OF AUNT SOPHRONIA

KITCHEN POETICS

*A woman who could read the Georgics ought not to burn
her beefsteak.*

Aunt Sophronia,
The Complete Home

The same female intelligence is at work
construing shepherds and roasts,
each basking in his own thick juice.
You could take it further.
How about rondeaus to raise the pastry,
pantoums for spicing a curry,
elegies for braising the innocent lamb,
and nothing but an ode when the table is laid
for more than eight.
Only our blue-stocking Sophronia
could dream such harmony.
The book and the pan,
the poem and the body,
the words in the blood, rising.

CLEANLINESS

"Nine months of the year our windows should stand
broadly open for a sunbath."
"But, my dear Miss Sophronia, it ruins the carpets."

Aunt Sophronia to Mrs. Black,
The Complete Home

Aunt Sophronia whistles through these pages
like a pure wind, sal-soda, ammonia, lime
a furious wake behind her.
Here lie the fetid syllables.
Soap-grease firkin, swill pail, cistern.
And those peculiar penchants of hers;
sinks and drains, bodies covered in flannel,
spore-ridden carpets, potatoes sprouting in the cellar.
The importance of removing those tuberous limbs
and carrying them off, to where she doesn't say.

Though I see her with a cloth full of pale amputations,
casting them over the water. Some superstitious softening
around those scoured edges, where God strikes
sloppy households dead and women who insist
on dark parlours and wasp waists
deserve the slow fires of consumption.

A housekeeper needs the hundred eyes of Argus,
warns Sophronia. *Shut up rooms breed pestilence!*
In her own home, she inhales the sparkle
of every cranny, each curve of her resplendent drains.
What danger dirty suds? cry the ignorant
flinging washing water across the yard.

Sophronia knows. God is a cake of soap,
kettle-cloths boiled to brilliance.
He lives in the light of her rooms
where she sits with the Good Book, praying.

A FINE ART

"Don't sneer, Helen, and mumble that it is 'vulgar,
common knowledge'; housekeeping is not vulgar: it is a
fine art; it grasps with one hand beauty, with the other
utility; it has its harmonies like music, and its order like
the stars in their courses."

Aunt Sophronia,
The Complete Home

Unkempt bird perched
on our house, dirt of days
clocking our hours. Old squawk.
There are better things to do.
Yet the bird persists
and the broom goes up the hall,
the brush swipes at the well of water
where our bodies' bread exits daily, there is
no escaping. So why not Art?
Why not call it fine and hear the music
with the folding and the putting, or plug
some machine into the wall and look
to the heavens, believing
the balls up there perfectly aligned,
beause you are doing
not what you want to do but
what you must.

IN CASE YOU THOUGHT YOU COULDN'T

*She had carelessly mistaken a poison given her for a bath,
and used it internally. My sister was baking sponge cake,
and had by her a plate of whites of eggs, which she was
about to beat. She promptly administered these, and
saved the young woman's life.*

Aunt Sophronia,
The Complete Home

There is no such thing as a disaster. Shake your broom at it, roll the
burning child in carpets. Mad dogs, sunstroke, runaway horses.
Presence of mind and cake baking will see you through. Remember
the boy with glass in his eye, the baby choking on a thimble. Think of
the child who fell down the well, the circle of heaven his hands reach
for, a powder blue confection he cannot touch. Bake plenty of cakes.
Bake them high and round. Mix half a cup of flour and half a cup of
table salt into a thick paste with cold water. Apply to the burned arm.
Slip three flax seeds under the eyelid. Think calm. Think Feather
Cake, Gold Cake, Jenny Lind Cake, Mrs. Holmes' Liberty Cake. Apply
poultices of mustard, of boiled hops, of equal parts hog's lard and gun-
powder. Doesn't matter what colour the child is; purple, blue or
aflame. Look reasonably at all things. Lower the mother down on a
rope, down through the well's silence, the unastonished angel, icing
sugar dusting her clothes.

THE LOVES OF AUNT SOPHRONIA

*If a boy can bury a chipmunk when it is dead, he can plant
a gladiolus.*

Aunt Sophronia,
The Complete Home

The culinary love of mock macaroni, made from broken crackers;
invalids in white-washed rooms; making invalids eat mock macaroni;
the maternal love of little girls with short-cropped hair not afraid of
touching beetles; the frugal love of all darning, patching, mending; the
familial love of three nieces, Hester the scholar, Miriam the home-
maker and little Helen, vain and indolent; especially Helen because
she is such a fine example of how not to behave, dragging a train of
white skirts upon the sidewalk; the cleansing love of caustic soda and
ammonia; rubbing her chest, arms and feet with a flesh-brush when
she is unable to sleep; the bodily love of stout shoes; a well-trussed
fowl; women who wash their children's mouths out with soap.

What we never hear is the word itself. What we never hear is the
need for it. In the word's absence her perfunctory heart moves like a
muscled hand, sinews squeezing a rag. Thump of a sewing box shut
for the night.

AUNT SOPHRONIA'S BREASTS

Do not expose bare necks and arms to the evening air.

Aunt Sophronia,
The Complete Home

Were made of flannel.
Were cold as tubs of ice.
Were kept under lock and key
in a metal box in a drawer.
Blushed in a mirror, not once but
twice.

Were two small dogs, rolling
against her heart as she slept.
Argued over who was loved more,
who was mistress, and who was kept.
Had never sniffed cold morning air,
or felt the sting of rain on their fat.
Could not tell right from left.
When she wasn't looking,
smoked a pipe and donned a hat.

Were blind. Were round and wicked and
always sticking their nipples out.
Had never entered the mouth
of a child, hungry and hurt.
Always wanted to know what sex was about.
Were once told to be quiet.
Once kissed and begged to waltz
but said they already had a partner.
Were fragrant as turnip pie
on a winter evening, soft
as puddings of snow.
Hadn't the time of day
for prayer. Were very, very
lovely though no one ever
told them so.

THE PERFECT BOY

"Mother, my dear," he cried, "there is not the least need of
your doing what you dislike when I am on hand to do it for
you; behold, how beautifully I can pare potatoes!" So
jumping up he took possession of pan, basket, and knife,
and began peeling the potatoes as quickly and evenly as
his mother could have done.

Aunt Sophronia,
The Complete Home

Don't think he doesn't exist, this well-mannered boy, the darling who
leans over pots and pans like a tender vine in the heat of the
afternoon. Mother lets him hide in the attic when the boys come
calling, when their sticks and balls raise dirt in the street. Later he
will glide down the stairs, bend over tubs and basins, white hands
swirling round the grey waters, catfish in a shallow pool. To shell,
peel, pluck and scrub, these are instincts, his soft mouth coaxing the
strange words out from under the bed – *duster, pudding, meringue,*
crinoline, French china. His tongue holds each syllable like a
forbidden bead; it is enough to make him float about the house in an
apron for days, lean his long, muscular limbs into spit and polish,
whip the cool sea of linen through the air.

THE FIRST FAT MAN

It will be no advantage to your dining-table to be light and
elegant: it might break down under your first big dinner.
Neither should chairs be light and elegant: they might
crush like an egg-shell under the first fat man.

Aunt Sophronia,
The Complete Home

The newlyweds await him,
their white china full moons
orbiting the roast, hieroglyphs
of well-laid cutlery impossible to read;
tragedy? a wealth of happiness?
They fuss over napkins, salt cellars, glasses
so polished the wine shall be cupped by the mere air.
It has taken days to prepare, she
has taken two convulsive fits since noon.
He holds her hand, says *It will all*
be over soon enough. The fat man
moves slowly up the street, a portentous balloon,
stops to rest beneath a tree.
She thinks of all her fallen cakes.
Her husband of an old man without any teeth.
The chairs kneel like soldiers at prayer,
flowers bloom and bloom before them.
The fat man knocks once. The room
flinches to doll's quarters.
Chairs, tables, tureens, woman and man, who
should go first?

HYSTERIA

*For Hysterics or Hysteric Convulsions, rub the spine with
a coarse towel, put hot water to the feet, bind poultices of
mustard and flour on the wrists and ankles, and adminis-
ter ammoniated valerian. Remove all corsets or compress-
ing clothing. In these cases perfectly calm common-sense
is needed to control the patient; the nurse should be firm
and not too sympathetic.*

Aunt Sophronia,
The Complete Home

Hysteria is a dying art. Sure
you see glimpses here and there.
The mother on the bus, her bawling kids
who ring the bell at every stop.
The woman in the supermarket
too fervently touching the tomatoes.
But it's not the old-fashioned kind,
not the clear blue abandonment
of sense and memory, the undeniable
reek of lilac or gasoline.

Downstairs lives an unhappy woman.
Almost every night we hear the screaming,
the objects thrown at her mild handsome husband.
Sometimes we put our ears to the hot air vents
to hear it better, this vivid beating of wings,
the great black squawks.

And then we only hear her say,
They're listening, they're listening
and him saying *No they're not.*
Tomorrow I will be ashamed
to meet her in the laundry room.
The day will clear and she will step
outside smiling. Tomorrow I'll wish

for the century to turn back, where
she could fall upon the grass, shaking,
and I'd be there, the resolute nurse
plying a womanly trade
of teaspoons and unguents.

THE FETISH

"What have you to say about high-heeled boots – real
high, narrow French heels? We are always disputing over
them," said Belinda.
"They are among the most dangerous things in the
world. To these high and ill-placed heels, which destroy
the balance of the body, may be attributed a very large
proportion of the diseases and weakness of the eye, and
not a few cases of insanity."

Belinda to Aunt Sophronia,
The Complete Home

You were hoping she'd cite a few examples.
You wanted to see the blind and the mad
tottering on four inch heels, wanted
to know the peculiarities of their bunions.
You think of streetwalkers, a game show
hostess, a school teacher whose footstep
was a timestable between the slanting desks.
You find yourself kneeling in your mother's cupboard,
sorting high-heeled shoes into perfect rows.
Your mother says you are very good at this.
She would never ask your brother, who is outside
doing something with grass and garbage cans.
Which is why you are inside on such an evening,
slipping your hand into small boats
that launch a woman over the floors of the world.
You marvel over each precipice, the lengths of strap,
buckles for the ankle's swell. You linger longer
than you should, float in the pedestrian smell
of your mother: leather, heat, sweet talc.
You might even be a little blind and crazy,
it is that thick and inviolate. You know you want
such a vessel, want to strap your heart to its gulch,
sound the clicks and stops of a language
you hadn't known you could speak.

Outside, slow clang of cans down the quiet street.
You rise to join it. The long lake of the parquet hall.
Your feet precarious; two thin white ladies about to fall.

MY MOTHER'S VASES

My meals always taste better for a bouquet, or a moss-
plate, or a pot of fern in the middle of the table. In sum-
mer we use fresh flowers. It does not take long to gather a
few and put them in a little vase or glass, and it cheers
the whole family up to see them.

Aunt Sophronia,
The Complete Home

Where others have not given
a second thought, you pluck
these ladies whole and shining
from the junk tables of Sunday sales.
The roll of a voluptuous lip, porcelain
bodice of cream, this one rich and cold
in her cobalt coat, that one slightly
mad, her green glass luminous
where an eye pressed close
swims like a startled fish
in a sea of cut stems.
One cupboard diachronous
with the tall, round, plain and pure;
where a hand reaching in
might pull out any family's past,
the dimpled silver gracing Sunday's company,
the miniature in the sick child's room.
How you let them riot now,
in the centre of your table,
like hands cupping
what is most dear to them,
cottonwood, lilac, branches of maple,
as if you always knew
love is this exact abundance
of shape and odour and disarray,
where the hairline crack runs
over the water, dark seam of use
cleaving us all.

AS A TOKEN OF AFFECTION

*Our Aunt Sophronia lives in one of our inland towns. She
is the relative of many of the townspeople – the Oracle of
all.*

Mrs. Julia McNair Wright,
The Complete Home

I often think of them,
Mrs. Wright, whose book
my father's great-grandmother
must have read, for recipes and
sound advice, and Aunt Sophronia,
whose speeches she either learned
or scorned. I wish I knew.

Sometimes in a doorway,
the author and her double stand,
a cruet set of oil and vinegar.
One with pale arms and children's
hands in the tendrils of her hair, other
that maiden prune of lonely years.
Wright kept her at her side, remedy
for the daily evils that beset a home.

The thick volume I hold, family relic
I scour throughout the day. For what?
For laughs, courtesy to the past,
and my own acid desire for what is
good and right in the days that fall
around us like a ceaseless rain.
Wright, Sophronia, unite within me.
Mix the gold, the bitter brown.
Dressing for a life I shake and shake.
The leaves drip and turn, I swallow down.

TALKING TO GOD

AT THE MOMENT OF COMING

Your body squeezes itself
so the wet animal of your sex
for one pure moment is thrust outside,
pink and glistening and naked.
Astonished by the bed, the rumpled covers
and the light falling through the window.
It noses the air like a small mole caught
in the golden day and so beautifully cries
for joy before you and beyond you
that you are too transfixed to touch it.
By the time you have opened your eyes
to the world again, it has slipped back inside,
beating for a while, a knock at the wall,
just to make sure you are still there, and
listening.

OVA

You know the old version, a battery of sperm
pummelling the egg's surface, tails lashing
back and forth, the mad fight to get in.
The egg, a moon of serenity, accepting its lot.
Now there's a woman on the radio saying
it doesn't go like this. Her egg is an owl eye
in the funnel of night, choosing her mate
from the millions clamouring for attention.
She sorts the healthy from the weak until one is found,
pushing dimly ahead like a bulb in a vast storm.
Before him, an invitation, the table set for tea.
She leads him in, the perfect seal of her side,
Do Not Disturb. Division roars, the new order
of the house. I think of the sperm crouched over
and over in the many rooms multiplying with abandon,
wondering how he ever got into this, *why him?*
And her fat glow, then, as the owl returns to her tree
wet with blood. The feast of the night
purged for her brood, their furry heads awake,
demanding life.

TALKING TO GOD

That's what we called it in high school,
lurching to the toilet after too much liquor,
kneeling down and spilling our guts,
pain, parents, all our unrequited love
falling into the white bowl,
the cold pale hand of our redeemer.

It made sense calling it that,
as it does now,
in the first months of pregnancy,
my husband sitting on the edge of the tub
rubbing my back and looking on
as I lean and yearn
over the circle of water,
speaking to whatever face I see
in the porcelain curves,
heaving as if to shake this small life out.

Why we ever thought God up in the heavens,
I can't imagine, for surely God would be
right under us, urging us on,
just as we ride a lover's body closer to death.

I feel a little older today,
my husband says, my *Oh God*
resounding through the plumbing,
to wherever God is
and why not in the sewer
like a huge myopic rat lumbering in our crud.
For that is how our souls are opened and read,
the ancient augury,
our voices above, whispering, pleading,
our insides pouring out,
the stubborn lives within,
moving, dreaming
beyond us.

FAMILY PORTRAIT:
AT THE SONOGRAPHER'S STUDIO

This is how it first was,
at seventeen weeks,
when the sonographer was busy
counting the chambers of your heart.
Your grandmother stood off to one side
saying she saw you waving at her,
and your grandfather stood to the other side
wearing the tie she'd made him put on that morning.
Your father leaned towards the screen
where you swam, skeletal, quick,
and with each move you made, swore,
with great reverence,
as if you were the most graceful player in the purest game.
I lay watching these three
who had somehow conspired to give me this fourth,
your bright life's hold in the deepest part of me,
my slippery fish,
until you are ready to jump,
glazed from the river of my blood,
burning for the open air.

GESTATION SUITE

1st Genealogy

We ask the woman
how she has grown
her fiery garden.
She tells us her land
was once a midden,
its black soil
blue-flecked with shell.
I write this to you
who had to come first,
small shell that broke
and spilled its meat,
so this one could grow,
a bloom in the hollow place.

2nd Botany

Kumquats. She has never
seen them, only knows
their name, two exotic syllables
to relieve this migratory nausea.
Her husband returns holding
a jar of dwarf oranges, bitter
disappointments. She settles
for guava jelly instead. The kumquats
are shelved, pallid bodies floating
through syrup. Somewhere in China,
a woman articulates *blueberry.*

3rd Economy

Frugal mound under jeans,
the first swell. I'd expected
something greater, a wallowing,
bassoon put to flesh. Quickening
is a lean tapping in my gut.

Pen scratching at a ledger.
Ten centimeters and
counting.

4th   Archaeology

In a dream the midwives sift
my dark boneyard,
arms deep in the red earth.
They pull from me
arcs of rib, lengths
of leg as rope is pulled
from a well, hand over hand.
I am not afraid.
Only wonder how I could hold
such beasts within.
Who gallops there
without my knowing?

5th   Architecture

You have lit a room in me,
my walls taut
as a lamp's wire harp
circling the bare bulb.
Navel pushed out,
small skylight
in the white dome of flesh
risen from the hips
like a city I have seen
built on stilts, the boats
with the people in them
floating beneath.

6th   Gastronomy

The Hungarian trick
is to use a ring knotted on rope.
My belly beneath, a lidded pot
old wives predict. Tomatoes,
onions, handfuls of paprika.
The ring moves in perfect circles.
A daughter I keep inside,
the sweetest pepper,
stewing.

7th   Cartography

Linea nigra.
Line on my abdomen
carving a road.
Rivers of blue vein
mapped on breasts.
Stain on my forehead a country
travelled but not remembered.
At the equator, my hands
plumbing the ocean's depth.
Find another hand, a foot,
hard plane of back.
Terra firma ahead.
Scribble possible names
on sheets of paper.

8th   Cinderology

August and too many
weddings. I observe
the slender dances, rings
of gold. In the heat I roll
like an apparition of squash

between the tables.
Spoons against crystal. Kisses.
Bride and groom try not to stare
as I pass. Let them have their
fairy tale. Procreation will strike
soon enough.

9th   Geology

After we first met I flew north
to your camp, helped collect
samples of rock for traces of gold.
The tonne of your pack between us
in the canoe paddling back.
It was September, you said
we might see a moose
between the trees. My turn now,
pushing at water, precious weight
I carry, the magic stirring into view.

NEW YEAR'S BURIAL

I kept the placenta in the freezer
for three months, not wanting to let go,
as if, in the coldest part of our home
I could keep her as raw and furious
as she was with her first breath.

In the woods beneath the house
the ferns flame green in the night rain.
Our baby is inside, her cough
an excuse to keep her away from us,
as we open the earth to this other provider,
whose thaw leaves a patina of blood
on our hands.

It's the difficult moment of her birth
I hold like a relic.
How you stood with the doctors
and not by me. My anger
as you took the photographs
I would later memorize for every curve
of her new body, for those large hands
pulling her head into the world.

You dig the hole.
Show me one last time.
How the cord lies caught in the ice,
blue rope that knotted her life
in mine. Even now, I can't say
I did this.

I wonder what else lies
under that glassy surface.
Like mittens and toys
frozen in winter's banks, waiting
for the release of another season.

We plant you, old blood,
like a secret.
Move the earth with our feet.

FEEDING THE NEW DAUGHTER

Tonight I watch the latch that opens
your hunger wide. You are still shadowed
and crooked from my body, like a stick
pulled from the sea. Under the coral
hedges of gum lie teeth. Each will be
a white flare of pain to bring you further
away from this food so close to my heart.
I would have liked to promise you
a life without hurt but these tiny
beginnings already mark something
I cannot imagine. So let me promise this:
rings, chocolate eggs and coins for each lost tooth.
Kind woodsmen, strong wings and forest paths
you will learn with nimble feet. Let there be
stalwart boats, white rabbits and slippers
made of glass. Let me promise
all the things we've always promised
our daughters, as their mouths burrow
into us and the milk rushes out,
the deep sting of pleasure we find
in this touch, the mouth hard and ready
for everything we have to give.

DIAPERS

Backwards, diaper becomes *repaid*.
All morning lifting the lid off the pail
and thinking *For what?*
Acrid smelling salt of the bucket,
mound of cloth in a pool
of yellow water. The baby's sure
spill into the world that will not stop
until his own life closes, a tap twisting
into silence. Is this it, then?
After the wrapping of his body,
the soft cotton pressed to his tiny sex,
a mother's insistent cleaning of her child –
the brew of a tub, warm and redolent
as the first waters we crawled out of.
The world's demand not just for the boy
but the dirt pulled out of him,
whatever he can give to the bucket.
The thick beautiful crap of his life,
here in her hard hands
wrung and counted like gold.

CHILDPROOF

At the side of the crib, the baby's
moon face appears shadowed in bars.
Belts, tethers and straps. Slip guards
and spill guards, gates and outlet
covers and cabinet locks. You'd think
we were keeping a tiger in stocks,
not this little child pushing a wet finger
into every conceivable crack of the house.
Yet he is the one we are trying to save
from his own furtive prowling, as if
he were always on the verge of extinction,
his ivory fat bright with our momentary terror.
Sometimes in the dread silences
there is a rushing from room to room
to find him, where he stands perfectly
alone and well. The rope of his life
he holds like a master; and me, the little toy
on wheels, panting breathlessly after.

AT THE ECOLOGY CENTER

There were books and felt
for puppets and various
foods of a slug diet,
including dog poo
which the four year olds
found delightful and later
long languid cookies they iced and ate.
No matter I planted hostas
this spring and have been out
every day with scissors and bait.
My daughter didn't seem to see
the irony and I wasn't about
to point it out. But now,
in the rain, as she prods
a wet body, slick and grooved
as a prune, its eyes swaying forth
taking inventory of leaves, pearls
of water, the backs of stones,
I feel something. Black ripple of an angel,
my daughter dips her finger in.
She is the protector of this form.
Look how they gather
the world in their wake.

SMALL LIVES

Each day there are new captives,
new homes to build.
She hammers holes in the lids,
lowers grains of sugar, flowers, grass.
On her bedside table,
rows of wings and mandibles
rustle in the night.
I can hear them, she tells me.
She also believes them thankful.
In the morning there are gifts
you'd expect from the insect world.
Smooth brown egg, whorls
of webbery, a pool of bright green juice.
Inside the jars each purge
is a kind of miracle,
so contained and absolute.

The antennae focus and twitch
as my voice leads a peasant boy
into the terrible presence of princesses.
She is almost there, soon to slip
far away and under the stones
of a garden path. Inside its room
the spider gathers to a tight bouquet.
A beetle, voracious, at a leaf.
Beneath the compound eyes
my heart rises, a moth stammering
at the light. Why do I shudder
at anything so small?
My shadow's leap from wall
to wall; and her face calm
as soap or milk. A polishing
of wings and feet, beads of thought.
The night's black bowl clasped over us.
She listens in and watches
where I cannot.

GARDEN OF EARTHLY DELIGHTS

BARNACLES

When the waves come in,
after a long dry spell in the sun,
their beaks fly open and by the third
or fourth wash of brine out come
the little tongues, clamouring, clamouring
for the salt and wet, even before they are
safely under the tide, so wild are they
for the water. It is a matter of life and
death, you can see that, you can even listen.
Lie down and put your ear to it, hear a world
of kisses stuck to a rock when the blue mouth
comes near.

MYSTERY EDITOR STALKS LIBRARY

From the *Globe and Mail*, August 1993

He's been haunting the library
for a year now, pencilling over
the rough banter of spy novels
with the Queen's English.
The librarian loathes him, his small fury
over one word sentences,
demanding subject and predicate,
the margins of history texts
crammed with mini-lectures on the British Isles.
Our Writer, she calls him, though this,
you can tell, is said with a sneer of contempt.
You imagine her thin smile
as the books are discovered week after week,
how she takes them home for the hours of erasing,
bent over his cramped writing
and rubbing the page, amazed by such thoroughness,
the cross-referencing, the copious notes,
amazed really, that he has bothered
with any of this at all.

And yet he has.
As she bothers with it, because it's her job,
she's got to, though not only because.
You think of all those wasted hours
and begin to sense under the newsprint
the loneliness of this story.
Fastidious man and finicky woman,
how well-suited they are in spite of the rules.
And you start a different scenario
than the newspaper gives, where the man
is in love with the librarian; every word
he writes in the margin is dedicated to her,
the gaunt lady on the stepladder.
Knowing she will read what he writes
and smooth it away, as someone touches the lines

on her lover's face, is what keeps him at it.
And she, in turn, loves him. At night,
after erasing a book, her sheets covered
in the thin black scrolls of his meticulous thoughts,
she leaves one sentence untouched;
a syntactical correction of a loathsome statement
uttered by a character who chews tobacco and belches.
She writes beneath this, in ink,
I quite agree! and signs it – The Librarian.

And leaves it at that, dreaming the book
will find its way into his hands again,
her slender script a promise of flesh,
a whisper of skin on the page.

BOOKS

I've heard one Victorian lady
arranged her bookshelves
with a grand propriety.
Careful to separate
the male and female authors.
Who knew what might happen
if blind old Milton
was left to stand too long
by the wit of Austen?
What illicit catastrophe,
mingling between the covers
in the black of night?
I love that woman, whoever
she was, chaste even with
the dry pages of her books,
believing they were capable
of anything when her back
was turned.

Like when we were kids,
even before we could read,
closing up our picture books,
our thumbs marking the page,
and then throwing them open again,
suddenly, expecting to find
something changed, the young princess
dancing and carrying on,
when she should have been beautiful
and sleeping, the prince ugly,
the monster
someone we recognized.

Anything could happen
inside that book,
when you closed it.

Or when you opened it,

which is how we became friends.
Reading that line of Donne's:
God shall create us all Doctors
In a minute.
Abandoning our study notes
on metaphysical poetry,
getting drunk on wine instead.
Deciding that was the best thing
we'd learned all year.

You told me about the summer
you worked in a secondhand bookstore.
How you loved
the boxes of old novels.
How you took them out
one by one, holding
their wobbly spines,
shaking them gently,
waiting to see
what would fall to the ground.
Ancient flowers, small
crisps of leaves and once,
a seahorse, a gallant little man,
with a brittle chest,
riding the wave of words.
You gave him to me,
saying he was the sort of thing
you'd thought I'd like,
still intact after all those years
of living inside a book.

And you also tell me about the calligraphy
of signatures inside a cover.
How men used initials,
but women scrawled their whole names,
intimately, carefully.
The Bessies, Amelias, and Ediths.

Women not afraid to be left inside
when the cover closed,
and it got dark.

I'm learning
it's also where books open to.
Like my favourite book of poems.
Every time I take it in my hands,
it parts to a poem I love.
But finding the same book
on your shelf, it opens to
different pages, poems
I've never read before,
so that it opens into you,
showing me the places
you've been touched,
your hidden spots
I hadn't known until
the book showed me where.

THE POEM

I once thought up a poem, he says,
surprising the young woman, his wife too,
by the look she gives him.
Or maybe she's used to these moments of his,
when he is feeling particularly generous
having rescued the girl from her smoky campfire,
invited her to liqueurs and hot coffee,
as the forest grows dim, the tidal river
filling up behind them with the night sea.
He's proud of this camp, the split logs,
the kitchen counter fashioned
from remnants found in the forest,
and the station wagon ready for bed,
down bags and lanterns and Agatha Christies
they would get through by the end of their vacation.
And he's glad for the booze he's brought,
to hold off the chill after driving so far
to find a spot like this, where he wants to say
something beautiful into the night,
like *I once thought up a poem.*
And now that he's said it, feels a little reckless,
wondering if he can remember that poem at all,
so long ago, driving all night towards home,
the highway an empty runway under the moon.
But it does come to him, the two women watching
as he leans into the fire, reciting,

June. The twenty-second. Nineteen forty-three.
June. The twenty-second. Nineteen forty-three.

His birthdate. Which may have been the first words
that popped into his head, or maybe, the poem itself,
which he somehow remembers as being more grand,
but it's late, he's had a bottle of wine,
and he can see his wife's a little ashamed.
The woman watches him, bemused,
as if she'd like to say something, but doesn't.

How could she into his big, soft face,
so openly theatrical, still hanging on a precious thing.
And now he says, shaking himself a little,
That was some poem.
So you can't tell if he's admitted defeat,
or really believes it, the day of his birth
sung along the highway as a sort of miracle
he didn't know he could speak.
Maybe even then he'd shaken his head,
with the wonder of it, his large hands
coming off the steering wheel
and cupping some unknown factor before him,
in the emptiness of that highway, the light
of that moon, when the whole night was his.

THE LINGUIST

A linguist at a book fair is looking up
penis and *vagina* in all the elementary school
dictionaries. It begins as a whim, mild curiosity
to see what definitions are available to children.
He finds the penis, yes, its copulatory function
well-explained. He remembers coming across that word,
copulation, when he was nine. How it made him
ache for days, the thick slap of it.
But moving to vagina he finds no mention
of a slippery act, only tunnels and canals,
the womb at the end a docking yard
for some great vessel. He wonders
what girls in grade school are
being protected from? Their vaginas
as removed from sex as vaccine or vermiculation.
He walks from dictionary to dictionary
flipping through the P's and V's, weighing
one definition against the next, jotting down notes.
The booksellers are beginning to avoid him,
whisper down the line of tables that a creep
is looking up naughty words in the sacred texts
of the education system. *Clitoris, labia, pubis –*
female desire has been forgotten, or maybe
just escaped into the field, into the surrounding forests.
It shimmies up the trees with its bruised,
skinned knees and hangs there flushed with heat.
It will not come down though he looks up
through the leaves and calls. Skipping ropes
beat the ground with the sharp puck of words,
hopscotch squares stretch into infinity.
He is nine years old again, on a gravel field,
the girls' cries like stones in the air. No books,
no dictionaries, only the raw sounds of territory.

GARDEN OF EARTHLY DELIGHTS

The sprigs of flowers tucked
into the kneeling man's anus
is what I like.

Our half-mooned vase put to tender use.

A posture learned in childhood;
head on the ground,
blind rump poking the sky,
feeling the whole world
could whoosh up inside
if you weren't looking behind you
holding that light blue Heaven in place.

We might be hard-pressed
to be so imaginative
as any of these hairless
humans, escaped into the still-life
of outlandish fruit, barely
touching skin to skin and
sporting such ecstacy
in every step.

That's why I like the flowers,
one red, one blue.
As if gardens could bloom
from our assholes,
for god in me,
and god in you.

IN THE ELEVATOR, A FART

Escapes a man, and he
pretends it is not his.
Even though it was loud
and rank and large he denies
any association. Clasping
his clammy hands together,
he watches the numbers
rise from one to eight. The fart,
abandoned, wafts to the others
on the elevator who, one by one,
turn away their faces and squeeze
against the walls. The fart rises,
palpitates the locked air, gaseous orphan,
and when the doors open, rushes out
against the wrinkled noses of shoppers
clutching their carts and children.
Their small register of shock as the fart
sniffs at them, its perturbation
at their perfume and soap, insides heaving
just a little as it slides over necks and shoulders,
rides on the tops of shoes and purses
along the circuitous halls of the store.
It calls out, *I am all alone,* but no one
listens. It is looking for a home. A father
or mother, its body soft with hope,
caressing here and there an ear,
a cheek, a newborn's blue unseeing eye.
If only it could go somewhere, even back
from where it came, but that is quite
impossible. The man already flying
headlong out of the city, on a train,
his bowels preoccupied with new
pockets of gas burbling within.

The fart, pale and exhausted, rests
for a moment on the shoulder
of a cashier, presses there

like an epaulette, her head
turned towards a customer,
she does not yet notice it,
smudge of something once opulent.
No one had wanted it, it had never
seen the sun or drifted through
the branches of trees. The cashier
senses a familiar sigh, her fingers pecking
at numbers, a sea of faces before her,
and she begins to look about,
as it moves into the hollow of her throat,
calling, *Hold me. Love me.*
Shimmering brightly for one sad instant,
dispersing its final, human breath.

IMAGINE THE FROG

Imagine the frog,
his wide mouth
and fastened eye,
the rich skin,
green as a bottle
darkened with wine.
Think of his waltzes
over the earth,
inner thighs
lean as white linen,
the slim hands
extending
to a sceptre.
Imagine the frog,
the damp magical sac
or terror-driven bone,
driving its nose
between your palms.
And don't forget
the tongue,
what pink precision
with winged morsels.
What stealth.
Listen Princess,
do not plant any kiss
on that fabled face.
Keep him as he is.
He will make you
happy.

ICARUS REVISITED

This morning the sky came with a warning; if you'd bothered
to look up you might have seen the red letters
cautioning, a notice taped to the face of the sun.
You believe in your good intentions; groceries to buy,
a baby to put to sleep in a high noon stroll.
You are not seeking any private act, and yet
the signs are everywhere. In the park a woman checks
her watch during the fortune teller's predictions,
the stony resistance of her face to the cards,
the gold-flecked blanket, the man's hands lighting
on love and surprise winnings. At the bus stop
an old man abandons a ten pound sack of apples
and denies they are his, even when a woman
insists otherwise, saying, *But I saw you leave them*
realizing too late the heat flushed face
under the hat, the sweat-soaked back.
Now the petulant whine of a child,
I can't, I can't, a young woman dropping
the young man's hand though he holds it out
as tenderly as a flower, the baby not falling
into sleep as if what she most wants
is too still and dark a burden. Perhaps you even
see a boy waxing his great cogent wings,
the day so full of things dreamt and undreamt.
At night you tally up the losses, count them
your own. Some you even finish, the failed
desire stirring a shock of hope. How easy
to take from others; the soothsaying clacking
on and on, the apples succulent, the impossible flight
finally articulate, your amazing aviary
striking the air.

CIRCLE JERK

It is this circle jerk thing that gets me,
a ritual of childhood I never had.
I imagine a group of boys on their knees
busily frantic in the front,
clutching their half-grown cocks
and groaning, smiling, doing whatever
they have to do just to get the stuff out.
I'm not making fun, in fact,
I think it's rather grand, boys sharing
like that, I think of their faces, the expression
of grief and relief, the spasm of coming
into the privacy of the boy next to him.
And I try not to think of whatever lies in the middle,
the cookie or cracker, which is probably a myth anyway.
But even this is ripe with religious intent.
The last to come made to eat the wafer shot with seed.

I try and imagine a group of girls sitting
on chairs doing the same thing. Their fingers
twirling under cotton panties, knees
flung wide, rosy nipples rasping against
their undershirts. It just doesn't work
and it's hard to say why. Maybe because a girl
wouldn't want another girl seeing her like that,
her face faltering and twitching and stupidly numb
before such ecstasy. It just wouldn't do. Or maybe
it would if only she had something to aim for,
like a cookie or a page torn from a magazine, but
what then would she aim with, how shoot into the centre
claiming the bull's eye with her cum?

With girls it wouldn't be a game.
But I wish it could be.
I need all the rituals I can get, so instead
I imagine six of them there, in a circle, legs
spread, their twelve knees holding up
a huge world between them, filled with

the pattern of oceans and ice flows and deserts,
their knees encircling the planet
like an equator burning with the same degree of desire.

And the last one to come,
the awkward one the delicate one the one who was so slow
and went through so much pain in getting here,
we'd give her the whole shining globe
and we'd say:
Here, take this.
Swallow this.
It's yours.

ACKNOWLEDGEMENTS

The poems in the Loves of Aunt Sophronia section were inspired by a Victorian book of housekeeping entitled *The Complete Home*, written by Julia McNair Wright and published in 1879. The home, morality and feminine virtues are discussed by a fictional character named Aunt Sophronia, "an indefatigable diarist" who imparts her domestic wisdom onto a small circle of townspeople.

Some of these poems have appeared, at times under different titles and in different forms, in *Arc, Breathing Fire: Canada's New Poets* (edited by Lorna Crozier and Patrick Lane, Harbour Publishing), *Contemporary Verse 2, Grain, The Malahat Review, Poetry Canada Review, Prairie Fire, PRISM International*, and *Room of One's Own*.

I would like to thank the UBC Creative Writing Department, George McWhirter's 1991/92 Advanced Poetry Workshop and his 1992/93 Thesis Workshop, editors Marisa Alps and John Pass at Nightwood Editions, Anne Fleming, Zsuzsi Gartner, Vivian Marple and Barb Nickel. Special thanks to Stephanie Bolster for her insight and thoroughness, and to my family for their love and support.